INSISTER

Ann Decter

gynergy books
Charlottetown, 1989

ISBN 0-921881-11-8

Cover illustration, *Insister*, by Dena Decter
Cover design by Libby Oughton
Typesetting by Braemar
Printing by Gagné

With thanks to the Canada Council for their support.

gynergy books
(daughter of Ragweed Press)
Box 132, Charlottetown, P.E.I. C1A 7K2

Canadian Distribution: University of Toronto Press

Acknowledgements: For reading and encouragement Patricia Seaman, Nancy Chater, Angela Hryniuk, Hélène Mino, Susan Knutson, Nicole Brossard and the organizers of West Word 3. For their generous support Irene Buncel, John Doherty, Rebecca Decter and all my family. Thank you.

The quote from Adrienne Rich is from the poem, 'Sibling Mysteries' in the book *The Dream of a Common Language* (Norton).

Canadian Cataloguing in Publication Data

Decter, Ann, 1956-
Insister
ISBN 0-921881-11-8
1. Sisters—Fiction   I. Title.
PS8557.E27I57 1989   C813'.54   C89-098555-3
PR9199.3.D43I57 1989

for Moira

The daughters never were
true brides of the father

the daughters were to begin with
brides of the mother

then brides of each other
under a different law

Let me hold and tell you

Adrienne Rich
'Sibling Mysteries'

ONE: A WORD

A word is a sound that is said, as in speech. An order,
a command, a promise. You have my word.
My word—
I want it back.

Sister.
A female, you, related to a female, me, by having one
or both parents in common. Both.
Common parents, everyday, unusual people, our ori-
gins. The sources of that family.
Mother, a woman in authority. Father, one deserving
the love and respect given to a father. Tennis love, a
score of zero. Not in love, scoring heavily in dinner
table debate, political entertaining, intellectual lobs
and skirmishes between crude language and prudish
values. A sexual war conducted along class lines behind
the barricades of ski holiday socialism.

A class act, act one.

Remember?

We were a family. A group of individuals living under one roof and one head. But not if the brain and the mouth are in the head. There were two mouths speaking, at least two that I could hear. Two brains itching furiously against each other. There were even two roofs. And one of them was hers.

But we were a family.
A group of things that have a common source and similar features. Thing, a person or creature, you or me. A step in a process, the next thing to do. The thing is, I want a different role. Like you have a thing about spiders, and I have a thing about being your older sister. Maybe a thing is a bone.
Dad, chasing me around one of their parties growling, "I have a bone to pick with you," over some prank with an old toilet on the front steps. We all have the same bones, having had a common source. And laying to rest a rumour I started about the delivery man from the dry cleaner's being Allie's father.

Similar features. Dark hair with early streaks of white, an inability to arrive on time, the habit of making long lists of things we know we will do anyway, avoiding conflict, a pair of big feet with hammer toes, a belief that good food creates happiness, the possession of money we didn't earn except through grief we didn't want, prominent noses clogged by dust cats and feather pillows, a dislike of being the first one to end a telephone conversation, blue eyes and skin that blisters in the sun, a nagging corrosive sense that if we had done something differently our parents would still be alive.

I have a thing about guilt, how it feed on a diet of oversensitivity and inaction until it's in your bones. I'm picking a bone with my bones and feeding them on action insistence and refusal. Resistance. Re-sustenance. Sisters. Resisters.

Relatives. Relative, meaningful only in relation to. To each other, to the meaning, to the relation to the connectedness, the point at which some thing in you meets some thing in me.

Bone to Bone.

Role to Role.

Positions assigned in the play of the family.
Elder, younger. I was born first but have no memory of your birth. My first sister. No memory of a life without you in it.

I deny my position.

I accept that for many years you were smaller than me. You wore the clothes that no longer fit me. But we arrived at a day when we shared the same clothes. Trading sweaters and shirts though my shoulders were broader, pants and skirts though your waist was smaller and I had to undo the button when I ate.
They fit us differently but we could wear them.

It comes down to bones.

Remember?

Mom said, "I have big bones"

Do you still want to be smaller?

We wore other clothes too. Clothes we made, clothes we made for each other. Made for each other.

Mom's clothes that held her smells. Tobacco, sweat, perfume. With crumpled kleenex in the pockets, that I curled my hand around in class, my hand inside her hand inside her pocket her smoke her perfume her skin. And I listened as Johnny Tremain's fingers were spliced together by molten silver. Even with those two fingers spliced together forever Johnny Tremain was able to alert patriots in time for the War of Independence and help found the greatest nation on earth. A crippled man.

When the boxes of Mom's clothes arrived there was crumpled kleenex in her pockets. I've got it spliced around my fingers, those big knuckles we have are rubbing bone against bone in the war for independence.

Clothes are still your language. A sister's language. The pantsuit I gave you for Christmas because it was off-white and shiny not thinking then that it reminded me of the blue satin pantsuit Baba made by hand for Mom.
By hand, her language.
In Yiddish or Russian or Canadian english.

The shirt you made and gave me exactly because it did not fit you exactly.

Changing buttons at the last minute.

Enormous changes at the last minute.

A woman is on holiday in France. Telephones ring across the ocean and back again. And she is dead.

At the last minute.

We learned to sew ourselves, each of us. Sewed ourselves.

Remember?

Mom said, "I can sew on a button" and laughed. She was free of that language.

I liked *The Incredible Journey* better than *Johnny Tremain*. It's a story about two dogs and a cat who walk hundreds of miles through the bush because they miss their family. The big question was how would they survive in the wilderness without the family to feed and shelter and stroke them.

And I didn't want to be the cat either. Feline, female, all the girls were supposed to identify. Small creatures with soft eyes and sharp nails who are clever in a selfish way and aloof. They make my eyes itch and my nose run, I lose my breath and have to go outside. Their fur is soft and their bones are tiny. You could snap them with your bare hands. Allie gets red blotches all over her neck. All-ergic. Alley cat.

But you know all that. Remember?

You brought a stray cat home and that's how we discovered out allergies. My friend took care of it while we were away on vacation and it ran away.

To resist guilt you have to remember. What you experience as true has truth.

A cat ran away with the moon.

I didn't kick your dog. I just pretended to because you fussed over it so much, feeding it scrambled eggs, morning and night. Scrambled eggs made with cream. And Mom defended you. Socialism with cream for dogs. When you weren't looking I drank it. For my bones.

A thing needs to test itself to grow stronger.
When you weren't looking.

How can cats have only one sex?
The other is invisible.

TWO: A PLAY

Act two. A head is also a director.
But we had two, with separate visions of the play.
We were acting out our roles.
To directors, to visions.
And a third.
A script we were devising ourselves.

You left young and quick. Uneducated. Took your education on another continent speaking english in a new
way speaking British, learning, like Dad said.
Said, "Get a good education and you can always support
yourself."

Daddy was a role named Harry. He was a man and he
was a Jew. He spoke army and medicine. Fought Hitler
with a scalpel and suture. Straightened bones, nailed
hips by the hundreds. Nailed to his pride. Of the money
he made. Of who he made of himself.
He spoke bones.

Harry, the person or creature, knew two things which I
am finding to be true.
You have to make yourself.
And "Don't let the bastards grind you down"

Bastard, an illegitimate child. Legitimate, ruling by
rights of heredity. Sons of bastards ruling by what right.
The old bastard was right.

Make yourself. Make a word. Sister. Mean something,
as my relative.

So when the old bastard was dying he was lying in his hospital bed he was missing half a leg his heart barely feeding the oxygen to his brain through his blood he was crazy his brain half-fed he was freezing he said to me Said "Just take your clothes off and hop in here and warm me up"
The old bastard.

Remember?

I like to think he died of a broken heart but I know it was his soul screaming to get out. I could see it in the bone that he didn't have enough skin to cover.

Skin to cover. Your ears. Put them inside your head. A sister.
Inside your head. Assist her. A word. A promise.

Listen.

Mom said. Said, "This is Heaven"

Where were we?

Listen. Your ears are the skin that covers the bones.
Her voice is low and gentle with no catches only moods
and lilts she says, "This is Heaven"

Standing in the kitchen she is smoking she is smiling.
There is Allie there is you there is me. And there is
nobody else.

Safety is a word not spoken. A promise. Freedom from abuse.

Two points a football player concedes when the opposition drives the ball into the end.

When I was nine I got winded tackling Charlie in a football game. Mom and Dad told me I was getting too old for football, girls had special organs inside that they needed for making babies. For breeding. I thought they were crazy.

I knew I was only winded.

A family was the physical product of the coupling of a man named Harry and a woman named Shelagh on the unspoken agreement that he would provide the financial currency and she would provide the emotional current. They would live in his house in his city in his country on his continent.

It was the mode current in their day. On his continent.

He cheated. She cheated. Football safety, tennis love. A second house, legally hers, a tax trick that he dealt and she took. Grand slam. She had a space. Safe harbour that lake. A lover, the other man.

Remember?

In the bathroom off Mom and Dad's room there was always a book or two on top of the hamper. *Sexual Politics* was there for years, along with Mailer's *An American Dream* which I read until I came to the part where he strangles his wife because she doesn't love him anymore. He still loves her, it oozes from the tips of those murderous fingers. End of chapter one.

Remember?

There was a skull in the den and its jaw was on a hinge so that the mouth it used to have could open.

Allie wrote her plays in the den. Her friends acted with her. Girls played with girls. And we gathered to watch, you me Mom. In the living room. The couch was the stage, the bedsheets were curtains the costumes hand-made the script was their own. And we always applauded at the end.

You helped with the costumes, didn't you?

A sentence is a decision. A judgment.

How can a species have only one sex?
Don't let the bastards grind you down.

At his end Dad was skin over bone that could not support him.
So small I could lift him in my arms.
I did.
He called me Allie until I said.
Said, "No it's me, you just think it's Allie because I'm being kind to you"

At the end they begged me and Charlie and Allie to let him die.
Allie and Charlie looked at the floor I said.
" I don't want   him living   on machines   "
and he died in the night.
One final red blip on the monitor screen like the tail-lights of his car receeding to leave you and me and Allie and Mom in heaven.
Kind to him. I was.

There's something I've been meaning to tell you.
Guilt is a failure to discriminate.
Hanukah gilt, money we accepted from our uncles to
spend on Christmas presents for each other.

Presence for each other.

Now.

Leave Allie and Mom in heaven, in that big messy house with sunlight streaming in the windows on a Friday afternoon in late spring, and Dad's taillights are receding. Gone fishing in the wilderness for a weekend. Freeze Allie and Mom in heaven, watching each other. Freeze Allie happy, unburdened. It's hard isn't it? Hard Allie, soft & sentimental. Hard, Allie, to have a baby so young.
Refusing. To be alone.

Fly back across an ocean to my continent. Sit down, on the red chair by the coffee table. I'll take the two green ones. Say you're leaving. Sit in Mom's chair and say you're leaving. You echo her and I answer in the past and present tenses.
The future perfect.

A sentence is a decision made by a subject.

A sister is a meaning in relation to.

Meaning a sentence I'm devising myself.

Cut through the bone.

A word is a sound invested with meaning.

You left. Mom left.
Said, "Goodbye, sorry about Allie"
Flew across an ocean.

Your bags were packed with words you thought you left behind.
Your trunk that we shipped from Toronto was stuffed with mother father sister brother.
And it was delivered.
A trunk full of promises.

Promises. Coming to the surface.

A promise, an expectation, some thing that can be relied on to happen at some future date. A relation. A reliance, leaning into the future.

Remember?

Mom thought that the end of *The Edible Woman* was funny.
The part where she eats the cake.
She said, "I thought it was funny" meaning it caused her to laugh.,

Meaning. It caused her to laugh.

Meaning. Purpose, significance, conveyed by language.

Conveyed by language from my continent to yours.
Across a bridge from the re-membered past.

Across a bridge I re-member the past it was a bird on my window ledge trying to come into my house. I made a sound and it fled.

A bird in the house.

Mom died that day.

Slipped away, on a foreign shore.

You were there when her bones were burnt to ashes.

I listened as the tide carried her away.

Heard the water lapping her up. Heard the birds flying over my head. The words flying into the open air above the ocean that swallowed her.

The ocean that separates me from you.

Sister.

It is a word that wants a meaning.

The bare bones. Naked and clean.

There is no more history. The past is re-membered.

Mom said, "History shouldn't be taught"

I was your sister. The subject of a sentence. The sentence is I was your sister. Related to a promise.

Mom said, "Sending a letter to your sister is like throwing it into the ocean"

A letter I've written myself.

THREE: A LETTER

Three sisters. Act three, no roles. Three sisters. Baring relation. Having meaning to me. Significance.

When Allie was nine she said "I'm going to be a writer when I grow up and live in a house by the ocean with three children". She has two and writes me long letters in printing done with different colours of marking pens, the pages are blue and green and orange and pink. She lives thousands of miles from the ocean and is terrifically sentimental about the prairies. Landlocked in an ocean of wheat. Her children had different fathers so the only parent they have in common is Allie. She writes stories with her children in them. One more and she's free.

Writing letters to me.

To me. A word. Sister. Meaning significance conveyed
to me by language.

That promise, my word. I am snatching it from the sky
where it is flying above the cliffs
flying out over the ocean I am
reaching out over the ocean I am
standing on the line of the horizon where the ocean
meets the sky like the prairie where I was born inside
the word, sister.
I am inside the word sister. Wrapped in a promise,
related to a word.
I am insister.

Inside a word where I'm searching for meaning.
Meaning in relation to.
Promise in a state of becoming.
Significance.
Signifying recognition. Re-cognition.

Re-cognize.

The woman who acted as my mother had a brilliant associative mind. It shone for me, moved me from word to word, from idea to idea, taught me to distinguish. To distinguish, recognize by a mark or sign, hear and see clearly, make distinctions between a role and a person, between kindness and manipulation, between happiness and wealth. Turn left and left and left again until the write brain is working to distinguish a sign. In a word.

Bone is hard tissue giving the body foundation. Backbone. Hard tissue.

Death is a sentence I am refusing to write.

Making a promise relate to the future. Making a decision a state of becoming.

The woman who taught me was a marxist existentialist.
A politician.
Karl Marx wrote. Words, sentences, books.
I'm collecting my inheritance.

A sentence is a judgment conveying me into language.

Freedom is a state of independence, self-reliance.
Promise is a state of becoming. A relation to the future,
a relation to action. In a state of independence, free to
make a promise to become in the future.

Wife is a relative term. Husband is the correlative of wife. Promises exchanged in a public ceremony. A future relation, each to the other. A state of becoming inside a relation. Inside a separate state.

Two futures that depend on each other. Inside a state, a correlation called marriage.

A state of dependence.

The women who taught me slipped into the instant between freedom from and freedom to. Forgot where she was headed, slipped into a marriage, and disappeared in an instant.

How can a species have only one sex?
Know where you are going.

Can I change the question?
I'm writing as fast as I can.

Judgment carries a sentence.

Recognize.
You married.
Promises exchanged in a public ceremony. A state of becoming inside that relation, the relation of a husband to wife. Of a male to a female, a female to a male, a state of becoming together.

Sister is a relation, a meaning in relation to a female.

Meaning. Make no bones about it. Too easy to be hard.

Relying on the word. Sister. Meaning conveying me into language. Conveying me into a relation between females. A search for significance in a state of becoming. A promise to myself, a relation, between me and the future.

The trunk is unpacked and the words are examined. Mother father sister brother.

Looking for meaning, when history is ended. The past is re-membered in a state of becoming. The future so close, it's almost beginning.

The future a question of becoming connected. Of bearing relation.

If I can't find our relation, what becomes of us?

FOUR: AN ACT

For action, act four. For reactions.

A play, this act. No directors. A script, this one, if two are writing. And to each other.

If not

monologue.

No relation.

Sand, drifting across the bones.

Monologue.

Sister is a sound.
Echoes in the desert of my mind.

Whispers.
Died of a broken heart.
Died of a broken heart.
Died of a broken heart.

So close, the future, adrift in the quiet.

Screaming to get out.

Kleenex, spliced around my fingers.
Inside, inside, inside her smells, her words, her voice.
Low & gentle.

Screaming to get out.

Remember?

A word is a sound invested with meaning.

A promise is an expectation for the future.

For action, react.

Make a sound into a word. Invest it with meaning.
Make a promise into a relation.

Act, conduct one's self. Write, form letters into a word.
A letter, forming myself in language.

From the heart:
Put yourself into language, sister, put a woman into
words addressed to me. Address yourself to me.

An emotion in the desert.

From the head:

A sentence is a decision.
My sentence is a sister is a woman relating meaning to me, conveying purpose and significance through language.

Sister is becoming.

Invest, fill, furnish with power.

Until there is meaning.

Freedom is a state of independence.
Of possibility, to create relations, to connect through meaning, in language.
Language addressing the connections.

Freedom is the possibility of meaning in language.
Of multiple dialogues.
A stateless relation.

The future is always beginning.

Always.

Actions for freedom.

From emotion to motion:

Writing is an action.
The women who taught me was an existentialist.
I've collected my inheritance.

The future begins from the past.

Flesh is forming on the bones.

Surfacing.

Life is a sentence conveying me into language.

A sentence is a bridge between two women.
A sister is a bridge-builder, a construction worker, mak-
ing the language have meaning for me.
For us.

Sowed ourselves.

Skin on the flesh, a surface of meaning.

From the hand:

My sisters are women who write.
A life sentence.

A promise, an expectation & the future so close it bonds with the present. Always at hand, the hand that writes and touches, sister, skin, flesh and bones of the writing body.

You begin again.

SISTER: SKIN, FLESH AND BONES OF THE
WRITING BODY.

A word always beginning.

Amy Gottlieb

Ann Decter grew up in Winnipeg and comes from a large, politically-oriented family. She has lived in New York, Gold River, Nova Scotia and Toronto. She currently works as a writer and editor in the feminist and literary communities in Toronto. An illustrated book for children, *Katie's Alligator Goes to Daycare*, appeared in 1987. Her work has been published in *Fireweed*, *Rites* and *Broadside*.